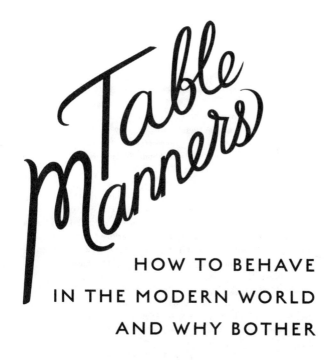

Table Manners

HOW TO BEHAVE IN THE MODERN WORLD AND WHY BOTHER

JEREMIAH TOWER

ILLUSTRATIONS BY LIBBY VANDERPLOEG

FARRAR, STRAUS AND GIROUX NEW YORK

Farrar, Straus and Giroux
18 West 18th Street, New York 10011

Copyright © 2016 by Jeremiah Tower
Illustrations copyright © 2016 by Libby VanderPloeg
All rights reserved
Printed in the United States of America
First edition, 2016

Library of Congress Cataloging-in-Publication Data
Names: Tower, Jeremiah, author. | VanderPloeg, Libby, illustrator.
Title: Table manners: how to behave in the modern world and why bother /
    Jeremiah Tower ; illustrations by Libby VanderPloeg.
Description: First edition. | New York : Farrar, Straus and Giroux, 2016. |
Identifiers: LCCN 2016007141| ISBN 9780374272340 (hardback) |
    ISBN 9780374714826 (ebook)
Subjects: LCSH: Table etiquette. | BISAC: REFERENCE / Etiquette. |
    COOKING / Entertaining. | COOKING / Essays.
Classification: LCC BJ2041 .T69 2016 | DDC 395.5/4—dc23
LC record available at http://lccn.loc.gov/2016007141

Designed by Jonathan D. Lippincott

Our books may be purchased in bulk for promotional, educational, or business use.
Please contact your local bookseller or the Macmillan Corporate and Premium
Sales Department at 1-800-221-7945, extension 5442, or by e-mail at
MacmillanSpecialMarkets@macmillan.com.

www.fsgbooks.com
www.twitter.com/fsgbooks • www.facebook.com/fsgbooks

1   3   5   7   9   10   8   6   4   2

To all those parents who care, and to any of their offspring who want to know. As well as to anyone else who is interested in how to behave to everyone's advantage.

CONTENTS

TABLE MANNERS

Introduction

Do table manners really matter? In his 1961 *Tiffany's Table Manners for Teenagers*, Walter Hoving says, "In this day of confused standards, manners are sometimes sadly neglected. This is especially true of table manners." I would go further and say: if there are no table manners, there are no manners at all.

Still, once learned, they should never become a rigid set of rules. They should never, as Hoving says, be "stilted, self-conscious, or artificial," but should forever adapt, though without losing their purpose: to help you get what you want out of life by doing unto others as they would have you do. When I opened Stars restaurant in San Francisco in 1984, I knew that manners would let me gain access into the circles of the wealthy and social elite of that community, to rally and enlist them as regular customers. Their shock at seeing that "a cook" knew how to behave produced enough curiosity that they were soon flocking to see what I had created. Good table manners meant I was all right, and, therefore, my business must be.

I have found that when people approve of your table manners they think you know how to do everything else properly as well. That is how you enlist them to your side, which is why *Table Manners* opens with a chapter called "Setting the Table." Here you will learn to manage the stage for your success. From there the book guides you through what to wear, how to serve, how to eat those pesky foods that cry out for fingers, what guarantees success at your and others' parties, and how to deal with eating in restaurants, both as a host and as a guest.

Table Manners is organized to give you manners for all dining challenges, including how to handle technology at the table. The chapter "Techiquette" tackles the problems caused by treating your cell phone as your dearest table companion and gives advice on balancing good manners with the realities of contemporary life and its ever-present demands for online communication. This chapter points out also that technology actually hasn't changed things as much as people think it has, and that the technology-induced makeover of our society is never an excuse for bad manners. It's not so much checking your e-mail that's rude; it's the fact that you've ceased paying attention to those with whom you are breaking bread.

The whole point of manners, especially table manners, is the opposite of pretension. The chapter following

"Techiquette," "Pretentious or Not?," shows that when any behavior makes other people uncomfortable, it's the behavior that needs to change, not the people.

In a world of increasing global travel, it is important to point out that, once you step on an international flight, many of the specifics of these first chapters no longer apply. The final chapter deals with table manners around the world.

Throughout, as appropriate, I've provided guidance for host and guest. Table manners are a two-way street—it's up to everyone to keep things running smoothly.

This book should be viewed as less about rules and more about suggestions. The world changes. But the general principle of good table manners will never change. You are always correct and safe from any embarrassing gaffes if you remember the Platinum Rule: do unto others as they would have you do.

ONE

Built-in confidence. Panic removed.

A properly set table establishes the tone of the party. It's the guests' clue that the host is prepared, that everything is under control, and that the party promises to be a good one. The table tells guests what kind of meal to expect—formal or casual—and how many courses there will be, so they can save room as they wish. Which fork or wineglass to pick up? The way the table is set is the guide.

When you look down at the table and see more than four knives, forks, or spoons in a row, you may be in trouble. You are eating with old money, or new who have hired an old-money butler. Don't panic. The safe thing to remember is to use whatever knife, fork, or spoon is on the outside and work your way in. With luck, those choices will coincide with the courses.

A thoughtful table setting puts the host at ease, too.

When everything necessary is already on the table or within reach, the host can relax. He or she won't have to keep jumping up to get something the guests want, and the guests are saved from needing to make uncomfortable interruptions, like asking for salt and pepper, which is an obvious public announcement that they think the food is lacking proper seasoning.

Setting the table thoughtfully, completely, and beautifully helps guarantee a relaxed and enjoyable party.

TWO

What TO Wear

Good clothes open all doors.
—Thomas Fuller, seventeenth-century
English clergyman

You don't have to be the best dressed, but you certainly don't want to be the worst. That being said, buying famous brands doesn't make you famous. Your own personal style and the behavior that supports it will do much more for your overall appearance than how much money you spend.

As the turn-of-the-century English actress Mrs. Patrick Campbell said, "My dear, I don't care what they do, so long as they don't do it in the street and frighten the horses." Good guidance for almost all social behavior, including what to wear.

IN ADVANCE

Dress Codes

Knowing what kind of event you are attending and what the host expects is the key to wearing the right thing. Hosts: informing your guests in advance what's expected will save them potential embarrassments and make for a much smoother and therefore enjoyable event.

WHERE

Casual Dinner

As long as you remember that "casual" does not mean sweatpants, any clothes that make you look stunning and feel comfortable can never fail to work.

Cocktail Party

The exact definition of "cocktail attire" is murky at best, but it probably doesn't mean jeans, unless you are positive that everyone will be wearing them. A good host will be a little more specific. A guest in doubt can ask the host in advance.

Corporate Lunch or Dinner

Dress up a bit when the host is the boss or the lunch is in the corporate boardroom. You may be judged ambitious for wearing what will impress the boss, but that works a lot better than being seen as unaware or sloppy.

Formal Dinner

Often means black tie and evening gowns. When it doesn't, a simple black dress will work for women. For men, a dark suit with or without a tie, depending on the age and background of the host. There are those who still think you can only wear solid-color shirts at night, not striped. I am not one of them.

Restaurant

Avoid those uncool moments of having to slip on a hideous coat-check tie or ill-fitting and threadbare jacket by knowing a restaurant's dress code in advance.

Someone's Home

Competing in style or riches with your host cannot go anywhere good. If you show up at someone's home covered in diamonds or sporting that new gold Rolex when the host is in jeans and an unadorned T-shirt, your best chance of avoiding offense is to shove the bling into your pocket.

Wedding Reception

The days of Royal Ascot top hats and gloves for a hot August wedding's outdoor reception may *not* have disappeared along with the horse and buggy, and guests have little choice but to follow the invitation's dress code. Hosts, please have mercy on the guests. The more comfortable they are, the happier the event will be.

WHAT

Knowing the event and what the host expects is success. You can always delete a jacket, tie, or jewelry. But you can't add them if you've left them at home. If in doubt, show up a bit more formal than you think you might need to be—then edit.

Belts

If you have to keep your pants up with a belt, choose one not just for support, but for color, texture, and the beauty of various (legal) animal skins. If you don't like belts, use that rack full of unused ties. Perfect for a picnic, beach, garden party, tennis, or any place with style.

Grooming

No matter how eccentric, grunge trendy, or geek casual, dirt is never an effective social message. If that's your message, no one cares. Pulling it all together should always be in private or alone, with someone else giving advice if necessary. If you are plucking your eyebrows or clipping your nails in public, it makes me feel like we should have first been introduced, and then interested.

Handkerchief

The common cold doesn't care if you need time to remember where you put the handkerchief and then extricate it.

The fastest retrieval is from the breast pocket or an easily unlatched evening bag.

Jackets
Men: Take a jacket if in doubt. It can always go over the back of the chair.

Jewelry
Saying "never wear too much jewelry" is as useful as saying that Carmen Miranda should never have had fruit on her head. Or that Lady Gaga should stick to one strand of simple pearls. No point competing, since there is always someone richer and more beautiful somewhere in the crowd. Wear what makes you look great!

Perfumes
Never at a wine tasting, because wines can't compete, no matter how great or expensive the bottle. Otherwise, wear whatever scent makes you smell good, enticing, interesting, and not like a department store cosmetics counter.

Sandals
Only Birkenstock lovers consider sandals a serious option for all occasions. Even then, please, no socks. And sockless espadrilles always work.

Sleeves

For men, it's better to wear long sleeves you can roll up if it's too hot. With short ones, you're stuck with what you've got.

Socks

Another beacon of a man's style, almost as much as shoes. A perfect place for a bit of personality, but never with hair showing above the top of the socks. Long white socks with white shorts went out with the British Raj and the Newport Vanderbilts, but they do make geeky chicken legs look substantial and stylish.

Ties

Hard to know when a tie should be taken out of mothballs. Unless you are at the office. Then follow whatever the most senior man is doing. Maybe.

ACCIDENTS

Holes

Unless there's time to change your garment, simply ignore any holes you find. No apologies, comments, or stories. If you draw attention, suddenly everyone will be unable to look at anything else.

Lost Jewelry

If something fell off and you *can* see it, then grab it with as little comment as possible, since no one appreciates unspectacular interruptions. If you *can't* see it, and it is spectacular, speak up; there will be at least one person who loves a hunt. The amount of fuss appropriate depends on the amount of money or emotional attachment involved.

Popped Button

Whether it happens on the way to the event or at it, if anyone notices just say, "Well, that's inconvenient," and move on. Pocket the button if you catch it. If it's on the floor, leave it unless it's a diamond.

Spills and Drips

Unlike with holes, ignoring a mess you make will give it unwarranted importance. Use a napkin dipped nonchalantly in your water glass to clean up your shirt, tie, lapel, or skirt. If the mess is food on the table and small, scoop it with a utensil up onto your bread plate. Or, at a restaurant, where you can easily get another napkin, use one to scoop.

TABLE MANNERS

THREE

And how to be served.

COURSES

Snacks

Do guests need to eat before a meal because they missed breakfast and lunch? Or because "appetizers" get mouths watering and juices flowing, ramping up the level of excitement for what is to come? Or to help soak up the cocktails? Whatever the reason, wow them right away, but don't overwhelm them or stuff them so much that the rest of the food goes unnoticed or uneaten.

First Course

Make it easy on yourself, so the guests enjoy a smooth operation: something already made, like a soup. Or a cold course already plated up to thirty minutes in advance, covered, and put in the fridge until you're ready to serve.

But don't plate a soup in advance: dry soup will stick around the edges.

Main Course

Cooking the main course "to order" means you will be away from your guests unless you are all eating in the kitchen. If you don't want to be out of sight and conversation with your guests, make the main course in advance: a roast that needs to sit, or stews that improve with time.

Dessert

This course can be the one on which you spend the most time away from your guests, because they are already happy and have found someone other than you with whom to talk. Or have dessert done ahead of time. Serve ice cream, for instance, and let guests help themselves to sauces.

Afterward

Sometimes an after-dinner wine (port, sherry, or my favorite, Muscat de Beaumes de Venise) may replace a dessert course. Serve with cookies, almonds, warm pistachios, or walnuts.

HOW TO SERVE

Buffet Service

For large, informal events, buffet service can be stress-free for the host once the buffet is set up, and for the guests

because buffets avoid questions of who eats first and whether or not seconds are appropriate.

HOW MUCH: As a guest, you don't have to take all the food you think you want on the first go. It's acceptable to get in line again. You are not greedy. You just don't like salad on top of your lemon pudding. If you do, get it all at once. Then you look greedy, but you got what you wanted.

PLATES: Hot, cold, or room-temperature plates, depending on the temperature of the food.

THE LINE: When to get in the line? Usually, everyone hesitates to go first, and then the person with the best manners will take pity on the frustrated host and jump in to start the line. If you are the host, you can always ask a trusted friend to start.

SERVING UTENSILS: Provide exclusive utensils for each dish. Whether guest or host, don't mix the chicken-liver utensil with the shrimp-salad one. And really don't mix the nut or shellfish utensils with any others—unless you are on the spot when someone drops to the floor, are good at CPR, and have an epinephrine syringe to take care of the resulting anaphylactic shock.

THE BUFFET TABLE: Can be set with all the usual flowers and candles and more, but the best décor is plentiful, beautiful food. That's what is going to wow the crowd.

WHEN TO START: Start eating when you get back to your place. Who eats first in this obviously informal event is not important.

Family-Style Service

Usually this means a bunch of foods in bowls or on platters put on the dining table in a restaurant or at home, the idea being that everyone helps himself or herself. Many claim that this dining style encourages interaction and creates a warm and inviting atmosphere, and it's often easiest for the host. As long as everyone's good table manners control any instinct to grab.

ALTERNATIVE: When the dishes are on a kitchen counter, then "family style" becomes, quite sensibly, a buffet.

CONS: A dire moment when the group is large (more than six) and the host hasn't provided enough food and multiple platters of each dish. The stone crab claws are at the other end of the table and start to go the long way around? What do you do when they are the only thing at the table you want to eat? The answer is: suffer. No matter how strong your lust, it's poor form to shout across the table to a friend, "Save me two!" while pushing your plate in his or her direction.

HOW MUCH CAN YOU TAKE?: This is a circumstance where you really have to do the math. How many are at the table, and how many spoonfuls of a given dish are on the platter? The answer determines your share.

SHORTSTOPPING: When someone asks you to pass the mashed potatoes, it may be a reminder that you want some, but it is not permission to grab some on the way. Not unless you have asked that guest, "Do you mind if I take some on the way?," and the answer is "No."

SCRAPING AND STACKING: Most people find cleaning up by passing plates to the head of the table unappetizing, but if that is what the host asks everyone to do, it's his party.

Plate Service

Choosing plate service over family style, platter, or buffet depends on two things: the physical setup of the party, taking into account your ability to carry it off without too much stress for you and your guests; and how many plates must be carried, how far, and how long it will take. Too long and the hot food will get cold, and cold food will be warm or melt. Unless you can get the plates to the diners quickly, let your guests come to the kitchen, pick up their plates, and help themselves.

PAPER OR CHINA: In the age of dishwashers, there is no excuse for paper plates unless they look and feel like china. I am a guest, and you can't be bothered with anything classier than paper? Hmm, let me think about that. Have stacks of china plates next to the food from wherever it's served. But paper can be just fine for children at a summer barbecue or picnic.

REUSE OR NOT: Use clean plates for every course unless you're a great cook who knows whether the sauce left on the plate from one course will enhance the food for the next.

SERVICE PLATES: Beautiful service plates are instant table decoration, and a fine place to put folded napkins. Then they become the underliners for the first course and the place to put soup spoons in between tastes and at the end. (See chapter 11, "Pretentious or Not?")

LOWER LEFT, RAISE RIGHT: If there is a wait staff, be prepared to be served over your left shoulder and for your plate to be cleared over your right. Anticipating this avoids collisions and spills.

WHEN TO START: If the host says, "Please don't wait," go ahead and start eating. If you would rather delay slightly until the people on either side of you are served, that's fine, too. When there is one host, he or she can be served first, so that everyone can start eating once served. If there are two hosts, one is served first and the other last.

Platter Service

In some houses and banquets, food will be passed around by a waiter on a platter served over your left shoulder. With luck, the platter will be low enough so that you can get hold of the fork (left hand) and spoon (right hand) if you are right-handed. Scoop up the meat or fish and whatever vegetables and put them on your plate. Don't press down too hard; the server may not frequent the gym. Put the fork and spoon back on the platter side by side, as you found them: this saves the next person contortion.

HOW MUCH: Take only enough to keep you mildly satisfied. The platter will come around again. Are you the only one taking some more on the second round? Not a faux pas, as rumored. Take some. After all, it was offered to you. As a host, you should always take seconds, so that all feel welcome to do so as well. If no one does, you don't have to eat what you have taken. Take a bite and have it cleared.

PLATES: These should already be on the table before the platters are brought around. If you're serving hot food, set them out just before the service. The same for cold. Plates for room-temperature food can be already at the table when the guests sit down.

WHEN TO EAT: Start eating once you have served yourself from the platter. It takes more time for this service than bringing in already plated food, and no one wants hot food turned cold. The host should be served first; that way, no one wonders when to start eating.

HOW MUCH FOOD

Quality

When food is perfectly cooked and presented, sometimes a little goes all the way.

Quantity

If you are feeding a horde of teenagers, quantity counts.

Too Much

If the guests leave the event stuffed and uncomfortable, they will think of you not as a successful host, but a blundering one.

FOUR

On what occasions may you properly eat with your fingers? As with most past rules of etiquette, the rules about such things as eating with your fingers have yielded to good sense. Here are some basic guidelines on how to keep your eating cool at the table.

BASIC WAYS TO KEEP YOU LOOKING COOL

Dunking

Everyone says you shouldn't sop up the last of the delicious sauce with bread. But Millicent Fenwick, in her 1948 *Vogue's Book of Etiquette*, says it is regarded as "a little eccentric, but flattering to the hostess," and sixty-eight years later I am still all for it. How eccentric do you want to be? Dunking is a good place to begin. Just do it with confidence.

Enough

Rules about finishing all the food on your plate start, and end, with your parents. Eat everything on the plate if you want to, and sop up the sauce if it's worth it. If you cannot finish that heaped plate of Thanksgiving food, don't. No one should have to eat more than he or she wants.

How to Hold the Fork

If you grew up with the European style of fork prongs-down in your left hand and knife in your right, stick with it. If you grew up switching your fork left to right between cutting and eating, that's also fine. If you were taught to hold your fork vertically in your left hand like a lollipop, stabbing the food to the plate, it might be wise to change unless you like having others make unwanted unkind judgments about you. When the fork is used for dessert with a spoon, if you're right-handed, pick up the spoon in that hand and the fork in your left. The spoon is for scooping and putting the food in your mouth, the fork for pushing the food onto the spoon.

Left-Handed

It's perfectly fine to switch the flatware and glasses around to suit your brain's programming. Keep the glasses in the order in which you found them if you want the right wine. Greeting those on either side of you before switching things around shows you think your companions are more important than a fork.

Pacing

It's considered efficient for a good party if you finish eating each course when the host does. If you can't see the host, watch when the people next to you have finished. Then put the knife and fork (or fork and spoon) vertically, side by side, on your dish. If the dish used is of a contemporary shape, you are out of luck: the flatware may not fit anywhere on it without crashing to the floor. Try placing it across the dish, on the rim.

Pits

The sight of fingers searching the mouth is startling. No one wants to see the inside of your mouth. Figuring out what to do with pits in this era without ashtrays is a challenge. If you're at the table, a discreet dry spit into whatever cupped hand is not holding a fork will do; then deposit it onto a bread plate. If the food is something like prunes for breakfast, use your spoon to take the pits out of your mouth and put them around the bowl on the service plate. If you have no such plate, then place the pits in a neat pile off to the side in the bowl. If you're at cocktails and standing up, spit the pit into a cocktail napkin or clenched hand and put this on a passing server's tray, but only if the server is returning to the kitchen. A potted plant is a good solution when desperate. If you're seated at a bar or a hotel lobby table, put the pit in a cocktail napkin and set that in an empty glass or, if nothing is convenient, your pocket. No matter how inconvenient.

Sharing

If you dig in for a taste of someone's food without asking first, then that person had better be in love with you.

Utensils

Don't use your utensils to help yourself from communal dishes more than the first time. No one loves the flu, and I don't know of any recipe that includes saliva.

Which Glass

No one ever remembers, cares, or agrees on what size glasses and where they all go. Drink from whatever glass is poured. I like the larger glass for wine, and a certain kind of glass for a certain kind of wine. Do what you want to. Just keep the wine off the tablecloth, the carpet, and the person next to you.

HOW DO I EAT THAT?

The two key points to knowing how to eat foods are: (1) avoid making a mess of your clothes, and (2) manage the effect you have on others at your table. If everyone else knows how to eat an artichoke, then follow what they do. If you do and no one else does, then you can help them out of their mess.

Most important, when you have style, everything looks intentional.

Artichoke

Eat with your fingers. Peel off the leaves one by one, dip each into the butter or sauce, and, holding the leaf by the pointed end, slide the bottom of it through your teeth, to scrape off the tender flesh. If the bottom of the leaf is tender, eat that. The used leaf goes on the edge of your plate or into a provided bowl. What's left is the artichoke bottom with a few of the tender and as yet unformed leaves still attached. Eat the tender parts of those. Scoop the spines out with a spoon or a knife and discard them with the eaten leaves. Then you are free to cut up what's left of the bottom with a knife and fork and dip it into whatever butter, mayonnaise, or sauce was supplied for the outer leaves.

Asparagus

Asparagus is generally eaten with the fingers: pick up each spear at the bottom end and eat whatever is tender, starting with the tip. The English think it's fine to hold the spear above one's head and lower it into one's mouth. In the United States, this is a bit extreme, but a lot of fun.

Do it if you want. If the asparagus is served warm with a lot of sauce, such as hollandaise, the finger method is a potential mess. Use a knife and fork.

Bacon

Cutting rashers of American crispy bacon with a knife and fork means the bacon ends up across the table or on the floor and not in your mouth. Which is why we use fingers to pick it up. However, picking up a rasher of limply cooked European bacon could mean that most of the fat ends up in your sleeve.

Birds

"With your fingers. Just tear them apart," said Martha Stewart of quail. Chasing a whole squab around your plate can be embarrassing when it flies again, this time dead. Stabbing is the way to keep it on the plate. A fork pressed gently into the space between the thigh and the body works. Once it's securely held, insert a knife into the breast meat along the bone to take the bird apart. When you're down to the bones, it is okay to pick them up and suck on them silently. Put the enjoyed bones on the edge of your plate.

Bones

You can pick up any bones in your fingers to savor if it is an informal occasion. Feel free to take them home for

stock instead of simply putting the bones on the edge of the plate when finished. If you've got a bone fragment or a fish bone stuck in your throat, at the slightest hint you will choke, quickly say so and get help. The choice between embarrassment and death is easy.

Bread

BASKET: If the bread is wrapped in a napkin, use the edge of the napkin to tear off a piece. After all, how well do the guests know one another? Put the piece on your bread plate.

BREAD PLATE: If no bread plate has been provided, put the bread on the table next to your place setting, where you can easily get at it. Left or right. For the butter, put it on a piece of bread lying more or less flat on the table.

TEAR THE BREAD: Tear mouth-sized pieces one at a time, as you want to eat them, and spread the butter on them, or dip them in oil. A slice of bread the size of your hand is not the size of your mouth. If in doubt, try eating your hand.

Cake

If you are looking forward to eating the whole piece, don't pick it up in your fingers. A lot of the cake and icing will not end up in your mouth. A fork or fork with a spoon will make sure it does. Using a knife with cake is a sign that it should have been baked by someone else.

Cheese

Not all cheese has to be eaten on bread or crackers. If the cheese is good, try eating it with your knife and fork, like any other course. Note that on the communal cheese plate there may be different knives for different cheeses.

Clams and Oysters

Put the shellfish on your plate, and spoon whatever sauce you want onto each one. Pick up the shell, and use it to slide the mollusk into your mouth, or use the little fork supplied to lift them out of the shell. Spearing the oyster and then dipping it will often mean you have to go fishing for it in the sauce.

Dips

How do you keep dip off your clothes when the chip explodes? Avoid using any chips or crackers that won't survive the plunge. If they won't, head for the shrimp cocktail. No double dipping once your lips have touched the first half of the chip or shrimp. That intimacy is reserved for kissing.

Fries

Using a knife and fork to eat fries is a wee bit dainty. They are finger food unless they are soggy with some wonderful sauce or hamburger juices.

Fruit

Basically, there are two ways to cut fruit at the table. One is to hold the apple, pear, peach, plum, or whatever on a plate, cut it in half, remove any pit, cut it into sections, and eat it with knife and fork. The other way is to spear the whole fruit with a fork, peel it with a knife while holding the fruit in the air on the fork, and then cut it up. This takes practice and is the lesser known of the two methods, so beware of trying it for the first time at a formal occasion.

Jams and Honey

Who wants your blueberry jelly in their buckwheat honey? Or your breadcrumbs in the jam? Each jam or honey should have its own spoon. Spoon the jam or honey onto your bread plate, or main plate if there is no bread plate, and then onto the toast or muffins using your own utensils.

Leaf Salad

You can eat some salads with a knife and fork. With others—such as watercress, which is half stems—you spend a lot of time chasing the salad around the plate. When the leaves are attached to stalks, pick them up with your fingers. You may get some heat for this, but it is so obviously the least messy way. If the salad jumps off the plate and onto the table, just put it back and continue eating as if nothing has happened.

Lobster and Langoustines

Lobster is a challenge only when served to you whole. When it has already been split, anchor a lobster half on your plate with your hand, or with the flat of a knife when it's hot, and dig out the meat from the tail. Don't forget the cooked red roe, the white fat in the shell, and any green tomalley. Mix these into whatever sauce has been provided for the lobster. When a lobster is served whole, break off the tail, and then cut it open to lift out the meat in the same way. The legs, knuckles, and claws require handwork with crackers and shellfish picks. Once you have cracked them open, use a fork or a lobster pick to pull out the meat. Finger bowls or damp towels are a must. As are bibs or huge napkins.

Muffins and Popovers

Break these into pieces after removing the paper on the muffin if there is any. Eating either of these when full of melted butter is a temptation that surpasses rules. For a popover, butter it while it's still hot by making a hole in the top and inserting the butter. Wait a couple of minutes, until the butter melts. Same with a muffin, but slice that in half, add butter, and put the halves back together.

Mussels

If no clam or oyster fork is offered, look like an expert by forking out the first mussel with your regular utensils and then use its hinged shell like tongs to pick out the other mussels from their shells. If there is sauce or broth and no spoon, use the biggest half-shell to scoop it up and drink from that. Another option is to sop up the sauce with bread. Or both, if you like. There should always be a plate or bowl for used shells. If none is provided, a bread plate or the plate on which the bowl of mussels arrived will do. Put the shells neatly around. Finger bowls or damp towels save trips to the bathroom to clean up.

Pasta

Many think the authentic way to eat spaghetti is with a spoon as well as a fork. It isn't, but may be necessary for you if that's the way you've eaten it since infancy. Otherwise, put your fork into the pasta and revolve it in your hand to twist the pasta onto it. When you're eating other pasta shapes full of sauce, use your spoon to gather them up, and your fork as the pusher.

Peas

Use a spoon, damn it. And a fork or a piece of bread to push them onto it. The English will smash them with a fork and then pack them onto the back of it with a knife, but then for that you have to be in England.

Pizza

You don't have to be from Naples or New York to know pizza is finger food on any occasion. Pick up a wedge, fold it, and, watching out for scalding, dripping cheese, eat it.

Sandwiches

Fortunately, most of us are genetically programmed to know how to eat BLTs, chicken clubs, hot dogs, and hamburgers. Using a knife and fork to eat them is courting a disaster of mayonnaise, ketchup, mustard, and slices of tomato shooting out onto the table. A large stack of paper napkins served alongside is as important as the sandwich itself. When in doubt as to the stability of ingredients, eat your sandwich while leaning over your plate.

Shrimp and Prawns

In the Philippines and Mexico, where old-fashioned European table manners abound, dexterous people use a knife and fork to peel shell-on prawns or shrimp. Don't bother. Use your fingers to peel them and dip them in any sauce provided. Pray there is a finger bowl nearby or soon to arrive. The same goes for shrimp cocktail. If the shrimp still have shells, heads, and tails, pull them off. If the shell is hard, bend the shrimp in the opposite direction of its curve to crack the shell first. If no finger bowl ever arrives, a quick visit to the bathroom will do, or a thorough wiping on a cocktail napkin.

Sides

Sauces, relishes, pickles, and side dishes all need their own spoons and plates large enough to hold them along with their spoons. Saves getting piccalilli on the tablecloth. Common usage calls for spooning the sauces onto your plate and not on the food, as with jams and honey. This is also a brilliant way to avoid overpowering and ruining the poached chicken breast if you find out you don't like the parsnip purée.

Snails

When snails are served in their shells, there should be snail tongs and little forks like those used for oysters. Press the two sides of the tongs to open them and grip each shell. Remove the snails with the fork. As for what to do with all the sauce left in the plate, mop it up with bread. This is so delicious a moment that it should overcome any formality. If it doesn't, wait to see if it does for anyone else. Or make apologies to the host and dig in.

Soft Tacos

Unless you have an extraordinary talent for picking up an open soft taco, you may lose 90 percent of it. Gently maneuver your thumb and four fingers under the taco to fold and gather it up. Bend low over the plate, and open wide. Your best chance is to eat half of it at the first bite. You can't be shy or hesitant unless you want your sleeve full of grilled grouper and radish salsa.

Soup

THE BOWL: If a soup plate or bowl is used instead of a cup, as the soup gets down to the last few mouthfuls and the plate is emptying out, tip it away from you and scoop up the last mouthfuls with the side of the spoon. If you mistakenly tilt the plate toward you, the gazpacho is sure to end up in your lap.

THE SPOON: The large soup spoons of yesteryear are now considered pretentious, but they do work better than their smaller and shallower contemporary cousins. Less dribble, less spill. Holding the spoon properly will keep the gazpacho from splashing around, whether you get your mouth around a soup spoon on the front or the side edge. Hold the spoon with your thumb on top of the handle and your index and middle finger underneath it for the best results.

FINISHED: Put the spoon between the soup plate, cup, or bowl and the plate that underlies it. Otherwise, no one can be certain you have finished. If there is no underlying plate, put the spoon in the soup plate and be prepared to say, "I'm finished, thank you."

Steaks

As soon as cowboys drove Jeeps instead of wagons, that old rubbish about "fork-tender" no longer indicated quality beef. If you can cut any grilled steak other than a USDA prime filet with a fork, it's rotten. For most beef, steak knives make life easier, more graceful, and certainly more enjoyable.

FIVE

Conversation

A conversation is a dialogue, not a monologue.
—Truman Capote

Whenever you dine with others, if the purpose is to enjoy the conversation and company, the food can be just okay. It really isn't about what's served, but, rather, the guests, the décor, and the conversation. If the conversation is lackluster, you might as well eat alone off a tray in front of *Game of Thrones*.

A lunch that the Hollywood star Merle Oberon gave in Acapulco in the late 1950s provides a great example of how memorable a meal can be with even the most ordinary food. The kitchen had turned out a disaster. With maximum aplomb and minimal fuss, Oberon substituted last-minute Kentucky Fried Chicken as the new menu—a move that inspired more than usually brilliant conversation.

The guests found the hostess's cool so captivating that they all recorded it at length and admiringly in their respective diaries.

BEFORE DINNER

Greet the Hosts

It might not be the hosts who open the door for you (it might be another guest, or the door may be ajar), so it's wise to have an idea what your hosts look like if you don't already know. If the hosts are not at the door, head straight toward them. If you don't know them well, that means they don't know you well, either. Be sure to greet them with your full name when you say hello. Walking across the room, you may encounter children, pets, or flowers. All are appropriate things to compliment if you are wondering what to say.

Don't Cling

Once you've finished greeting or introducing yourself to the host, keep moving: it's time to turn to the other guests. If you're super-motivated, you might be wise to research them, and have a handful of conversation openers in your pocket. It's never appropriate to ask who else will be there before you accept an invitation, so you might not know anything about the others. Walk up to anyone standing alone, put out your hand, and introduce yourself.

See, Don't *Meet*

If your memory is foggy and there's even the slightest chance you've met someone before, it's always safer to say "Nice to see you" than "Nice to meet you."

Fetch a Cocktail

If there is a drinks period before the meal, offer to get a drink for the nearest drinkless and unoccupied person. "I see there's a pitcher of margaritas; may I get you a glass?" If the person is in a conversation when you get back, all the better: now he or she can introduce you to the other guest. Excusing yourself to go get another drink is also the best way to wander off and meet another group when you are ready to exit the current conversation.

AT DINNER

Once Seated

If seated next to guests you don't know, the first thing is to introduce yourself. When they start to ask you questions, it's always best to have responses in mind for "What do you do?" and "Where are you from?" Better to make up something fun than to drone on if you aren't capable of answering briefly. Try to avoid asking these questions yourself; instead, attempt to get the conversation to a topic that will allow both parties to contribute. The peril of questions like "What do you do?" is not just that they invite a monologue; they can also kill conversation. I once asked a leading New York City forensic pathologist specializing in violent *Scarface*-type murders about his work. He described a serial killer who had a fascination for crucifixions. The guests at the dinner had just been served rare and bloody roast beef. Some were quite put off the meal.

Pay Attention to Both Your Neighbors

There is no hard and fast rule about how long to talk to the neighbor on your left before turning to your right, but equal time is a good guideline. As for taking a cue from the host's turning from the left to the right halfway through the meal, this was fine in Emily Post's day, but the need to "turn the table" is no longer common knowledge. Instead, take a cue from your neighbor on either side, or be the initiator. The important thing is not to spend the whole night talking to someone on one side and ignoring the person on the other.

Group Conversation

If the host thinks the conversation at the table is flagging, he or she may address the whole table with a topic to grab everyone's attention—perhaps even something controversial. No need to jump in with the first response, especially if you aren't sure where the host wants the conversation to go. Pitch in after you hear some others and get the lay of the table. While a group conversation is getting under way, starting your own with the person next to you may piss off the host. Keep it to a few side remarks and you'll be safe.

Changing Seats

The host may think an interesting way to keep the party lively is to ask everyone to switch seats between courses. This is usually a major and unwelcome disturbance and rarely works. If you are the host, I don't recommend it.

De-escalating

If, despite your best efforts, your amusing and interesting conversational gambit is some other guest's idea of offensive, you may need to issue an apology even if you are unclear about what you did. The punishment must fit the crime, so anything from a graceful "I'm sorry" to an abject apology may be needed.

Interrupting to Voice Your View

You have a point to make? Best to get a grip and realize the evening will not crash because your pet opinion is not aired.

Interrupting to Serve or Be Served

One of the pleasures of eating in a home and not a restaurant is that someone isn't constantly interrupting you to describe specials, ask you if you are enjoying everything, or inquire whether you have finished. If you are the host, don't interrupt gripping conversation for "Does anyone want seconds?" There are always lulls; that's the time to offer more. If there are no lulls, that means the guests are so involved in the conversation they aren't thinking about eating more food. Congratulations! You are throwing a great dinner party. Don't ruin it. Motion with your eyes, gesture, or just pass the platters down the table. The same is true for guests who want more. If you are going to interrupt a conversation, it had better be because it's boring or because a political or religious fight is about to explode.

Chewing with Your Mouth Open

Everyone knows not to do this in theory, but be wary of times when a conversation point comes to mind and you haven't quite finished your current mouthful. However beautiful the food is, it's less so when half chewed in your mouth.

Listen

The number-one rule for enjoyable and profitable conversation is to listen more than you talk. Forget yourself and concentrate on the others, even if it means having to "listen attentively to a lot of things you already know." True for the playwright George Bernard Shaw, and true for us. Even if you aren't interested in what the other person is saying, fake it. Then you will often discover you were far more interested than you thought. The most effective way to win someone to your side is to leave that person with the impression that you found him or her fascinating, knowledgeable, and great company.

Eyes
If you engage everyone's, you control the room.

WHAT ABOUT

We never mentioned politics, money, or trouble
before dessert had been served.
—M.F.K. Fisher, food writer

Books, Theater, Museums, Television
All fine, especially if relevant to something that's been mentioned by the host or another guest.

Décor
What the table looks like, from the flowers to the glasses and plates, almost always works as an interesting first topic, because everyone can chime in.

The Food
Successful conversation about food in the new me-centered culture is more difficult than it used to be. You will find that whenever you bring up, for example, the curious life

of a Dover sole, sometimes all you get back is a quick "I hate Dover sole." Keep trying! Restaurant experiences, fantasy menus, recipes, eating sheep eyes—everyone eats, so everyone can contribute. And you really should find something nice to say about the food or drink you are being served, especially if your host has gone to some trouble. But comparing the food, even favorably, to other meals you've had will put you on thin ice. Your job is to be a charming guest, not a food critic.

The Other Person's Job
But not your own, unless pressed.

Weather
Still the safest topic when not boring. Much more an English obsession—and rightly so if there is a picnic planned.

Witticisms
A few witty one-liners dropped into the conversation can always keep the ball rolling.

NOT ADVISABLE

Grammar Doesn't Matter
Grammar is quicksand. When others make a mistake, let it go. You might well be wrong, and you will definitely be rude. It's never a good idea to correct the grammar or

word choice or pronunciation of anyone who isn't your child or your student. And even then, not at dinner with others.

Hogging Airtime

Once others are looking at their phones, they have stopped listening. So let someone else have a go.

I'll Show You Mine

Is there ever really a good moment for one-upping? If someone mentions something they like, that's not an invitation for you to describe something better.

Lengthy Apologies

Why explain, when good friends don't need it and your enemies won't believe you? So you kept everyone waiting because there were no taxis in the rain, even though you left fifteen minutes earlier than usual, and forgot your cell phone at home and couldn't call to say you were running late. Don't take up half the dinner telling the whole boring story. Did you just spill red wine all over the tablecloth? It's ruined, but so is the evening if you go on and on about it. If you are at fault, one effective "sorry" is enough, for all occasions. Even without the trendy and meaningless "so." Belaboring the point with endless excuses stinks of "look at me" and insincerity. If you need to apologize more, do so later, after the party is over.

Medical Monologue

Medical monologues are a way to depress everyone in hearing range. Stomach flu doesn't go well with food. Talking about its effects is even worse. When people at the dinner table ask generally about your health, resist fiercely the need and desire to answer anything but "Fine, thank you." They really don't want to know. Medical one-upmanship is even worse. Leave the organ recitals for the concert hall.

Stop Me

From saying "Stop me if I've told you this before." If you have the slightest doubt, ditch the story. Avoid being a bore. And if you're interrupted while telling a story, more than three minutes have passed, and no one is looking at you in quiet anticipation, once again ditch it.

The News

Everyone has seen the story at least three times that day on one media form or another. So, to be captivating, it had better be an approaching hurricane, a just-in presidential election result, or a declaration of war.

Travel

Place-dropping is as bad as name-dropping. And your vacation may not be nearly as interesting to others as you think it is.

THE VOLATILE TRIUMVIRATE

When the conversation sags, there are always these three topics. Long considered taboo, they often make for the most interesting conversations. But dive in at your own risk.

Politics

It can be fascinating to discuss affairs of state—if you are sure that everyone has the manners to stay calm. If you're at ease with your beliefs, let others be with theirs. And unless you are certain you are surrounded by others who like heated conversations, abort if things turn nasty. It's a dinner, not a debate; a time to learn, not to lecture.

Religion

As with politics, if you are content in your religious skin, let others be in theirs.

Sex

Sex is an acceptable subject when it is about other people, kind, funny, and spoken of with an air of astonishment.

LEAVING

When to leave is a whole other discussion, and we will address that later (page 78). But you do need to say something, not simply disappear (unless it's a big party and you are leaving early).

The Other Guests

Make sure to tell other guests, especially the ones you sat nearest, how much you enjoyed talking with them. If you can do so in the presence of the host, all the better. It will make your host happy to know that he or she made the right choice of guests. It's perfectly fine to have an extroduction if you can't remember someone's name and want to keep in touch. Just say something like "I am terrible with names, and I apologize, would you tell me yours again?"

The Staff

If it was a formal dinner, there may have been staff. Depending on how well you know the host, he or she may appreciate your thanking the kitchen and service staff. Just words—you leave cash only if you've been staying with someone.

The Host

Thank the host last, and keep it brief. And once you start to leave, go through with it. The hour-long goodbye is fine if you are emigrating for good, not if you are simply heading home. Say something warm, and be specific about the food, wine, or company. Then go.

SIX

Your Party

If anything is worth doing, it is worth
doing in style and on your own terms—
and nobody goddamned else's.
—Lucius Beebe

Even if some of your guests might think your menu choices odd, stick to your guns and just get on with it. Good food doesn't have to be fancy. If you are serving burgers, make the best burgers you can, and pair them with the best bottle of wine you can afford. Never apologize.

Your party, your style. But, that said, it's your guests' comfort, pleasure, and safety that are at stake here. So, whatever your plans for the event, think more about what they would enjoy than about your private whims. This will improve the overall event and make for a good experience all around.

NO SPACE, NO MONEY?

Most of us have been there. Maybe now, or maybe at some point when the pay was low and the budget was nonexistent. No space, no kitchen, no money for a big bash, no problem. You can still throw a party, even if it's an indoor picnic.

Décor

The famous French writer Jean Cocteau used toys from a stall on the street to decorate Picasso's lunch table. Anything funny and conversation-stirring on the table will do. Candles work miracles. Goldfish in a vase. The latest controversial photography book will spark conversation, no matter who the guests.

Drinks

Let the drinks do the heavy lifting. Even cheap vodka tastes good when mixed with fresh lemon juice, basil-flavored sugar syrup, and lots of ice.

Food

Plan a cold or room-temperature first course that you can cook the day before. A couple of hours beforehand, you can whip up a mushroom frittata, or deviled eggs with avocado mayonnaise. If you are running last-minute, asparagus or spaghetti with vegetables and lots of fresh basil from the farmer's market is a perfect save. *Dulce de leche* ice cream with rum poured over it will keep guests feeling fancy in the most humble circumstances. Vanilla ice cream with berries and store-bought cinnamon cookies will also be a sure crowd pleaser.

Kitchen

All you need is two burners and a fridge with a freezer for ice, vodka, and ice cream. Making soups or sauce bases ahead of time will be a tremendous help: one large pot for pasta, and one large nonstick frying pan for the omelets, and you're golden.

Menu

Keep it simple. That's the best guarantee of success, and the least headache for you.

Space

If there's no room for a table, use tray tables or put a "buffet" in the kitchen. Guests will be happy to come in and help themselves.

COCKTAIL PARTY

Two hands are rarely enough at a cocktail party. Guests need one hand for the drink, and one for the plate of food. The host planning for how guests can also hold a napkin, shake hands, or reach for a handkerchief while managing a drink and food will help make for a memorable party, not one that everyone wants to leave.

Food

COCKTAIL NAPKINS: Keep napkins stacked next to the food so guests don't have to worry about shaking hands dripping in ketchup. Also stacks at the bar and around the room.

DISCARDS: No one wants to be left holding toothpicks, Chinese soup spoons, or skewers. Provide tables around the room with discard containers for these, and for snacks people reject.

ONE BITE: Don't serve anything that is more than a comfortable one-bite or it may end up down the front of a guest. A lamb chop, no matter how petite, is not an hors d'oeuvre.

NOT HOT: Never serve food hot enough to burn anyone's mouth.

SAUCES: Set these out in bowls on a tray with a place to put the used skewers or toothpicks.

SMELL: Crab salad is one thing, crab breath another. Guests want to eat what they choose, not what they smell on another's breath. Never use ingredients that linger, no matter how delicious.

TEXTURE: Crackers or brittle toast will burst and dump the shrimp salad down the front of your guests' cashmere. Pick things that will save yourself and your guests a mess.

Drinks

If you want to feature two of your favorite cocktails or make pitchers of sangria, then do. Otherwise, vodka or gin and Scotch or bourbon make everyone happy, if wine is also offered. You are entertaining, not competing in mixology.

COLD: Have you forked out for champagne for the guests when they arrive? No one wants it warm: ice the sparkling and white wines more than two hours before the event starts.

FRUIT GARNISHES: Cut fruit garnishes at the last minute. Brown and slimy limes ruin a drink.

GLASSES: Make sure there are enough. Freeze cocktail glasses. Glasses kept out on a hot August afternoon kill a cocktail, no matter how much ice. Put wineglasses in the fridge.

MIXERS: Should be iced down—not like warm soup with an ice cube in it. If you are really good, the gin and vodka are on ice, too.

SERVING: Set up a bar so people can help themselves. You can make the first drink and instruct them to help themselves to more. If using servers for a large party, best not to pass anything but wine; if it's white, keep it cold, pass the glasses, and pour from a bottle. And best not to offer wine at the entrance or you will run into the problem of having guests who have looked forward to a gin and tonic now stuck with a glass of warm chardonnay.

LUNCH OR DINNER PARTY

Your being a relaxed and hospitable host is the key to your guests' having a good time at your table. And it's all in the planning. When you have thought of everything, especially which friends you will invite and how to seat them, you can be comfortable enough to deal with anything that comes up. Here is how and what to plan.

In Advance

COATS: Beds work. For a big party, hire a coat rack and someone to supervise it. Prevents a wonderful occasion from turning sour at the end.

INVITING PEOPLE: Thinking of your guests' needs is key when inviting them. Whether by phone, e-mail, or mail, remove all invitees' possible anxieties by saying up front what kind of event you are having. And mention anything else expected of them, such as what they should wear if that's important to you. If it's everything from blue jeans to black tie, say so. As for timing, the British custom of saying "seven-thirty for eight" is very clear. It means "Please don't arrive before seven-thirty," and that guests can properly arrive up to a couple of minutes before eight, when drinking stops and dinner is served. Let's all adopt that system. Mentioning the end time for a cocktail party is just as essential. Also, don't leave anyone hanging as to the nature of the event: if the invitation is for 6:00 p.m., is it cocktails or a dinner? And it's important to note that it's not nice to invite people who you know hate one another, or who are going through an acrimonious divorce.

KIDS: Special food for the kids? Not unless it's their party or they outnumber you. In which case, run.

LISTS: Being prepared is not just the Boy Scouts' motto. Make lists of the things you have to do. It will not only ensure a smoother party to write out your "To Do"s for setting the room, shopping, and prepping the food and drinks, but will also alleviate your own anxiety.

NAMES: Being introduced to more than three people at once is when names go in one ear and out the other. Not the host's problem. All he or she can do is introduce everyone once. The rest is up to them.

PLACE CARDS: A custom of formal dining that should never be abandoned. Written not just on the side facing the guest (they know their names), but also on the side that faces out across the table. That way, at least two people other than the ones sitting next to each guest can cheerfully say his or her name when starting a conversation.

SEATING PLAN: The arrangement should make well-mannered sparks. You don't have to invite couples, and if you do, you don't have to seat them next to each other. They already see enough of each other. Put people next to one another who will enjoy that choice and create interest around the table. You can go mad trying to stick to the man-woman-man format when someone cancels at the last minute. Forget it. We live in a world of multitudes of fluid genders.

SPECIAL DIETS: A guest may be vegan (and you aren't), may not drink (and you do), or may be allergic to so many foods that figuring out what to serve may seem insurmountable. But one or two additions to your planned menu are a nice gesture to those with particular needs and can be store-bought if you are overwhelmed. If you can't handle needs comfortably, take the guests to a restaurant. They can surf the menu and eat what they want.

THE BATHROOM: No one wants to eat the warm chocolate-chip cookies with their hands now cross-contaminated with someone else's flu, thanks to the lone shared towel at the sink. Make sure to provide hand sanitizer and stacks of cotton or paper towels. Providing a container big enough to hold the used towels means less clean-up for you.

The Room

If the table is beautiful, the room doesn't have to be.

FLOWERS: Flowers arranged above or below sight lines prevent guests from having to lean over to make eye contact with the beauty across the table. Choose non-fragrant flowers, to allow full appreciation of the wines. Even if fragrant old roses are your pride and joy from the garden, you don't want them competing with your pinot noir.

MUSIC: Having the music on when the guests arrive is a good way to set the mood. Best to set a playlist beforehand, so that there is no interruption in the flow. And if your friends are hard of hearing, keep the music low.

TABLE DÉCOR: Go crazy with this, whether the party is themed or you are just supplying a good conversation starter. At the press lunch to promote the opening of my restaurant Stars in San Francisco, the construction wasn't finished. To make a victory out of an embarrassment, we covered the table in the middle of the unfinished restaurant with hammers, nails, orange extension cords, and anything silvery in the place of real silver. It worked.

UNIVERSAL HOSTING TRUTHS

Some tidbits of advice apply to any and every type of function you may be throwing. Think of this as your hosting cheat sheet.

Be Clear About How You Want to Be Helped

Have you felt deserted by inconsiderate guests, or driven mad by a free-for-all of well-meaning but useless ones? If you want assistance, be very clear about asking guests to help cook or clean up. Pick one person to help you clear. All the rest, "Please, stay seated." You should feel comfortable saying to any offers of help, "Thanks for offering, but, please, let me do it. I promise, when I am at your house I will not lift a finger."

Drugs

If the guests start using drugs that are not on the menu or entertainment schedule, a firm "Please, no," is within everyone's bounds of best behavior.

Gifts

The art of receiving gifts is to do it without making those who haven't brought one feel embarrassed. Just say, "I can't wait to open this later," or "I will add this to my collection and enjoy it with you at another time," or "Beautiful flowers—I will just put them in water for later." If it's not Christmas, don't stack gifts anywhere visible.

On Time

If you want to talk to your guests and sit down with them, have everything ready by the time you said the event begins.

When No One Is Eating

When the food goes wrong, you don't have to do like François Vatel in 1671, the great French chef who fell on his sword because the turbot never arrived for the King's dinner. If one of your guests is not eating, ask why without attracting anyone else's attention, so that the guest will answer honestly. If he's just not hungry, let it drop. If no one is eating, serve dessert.

How It Ends

WHEN: The nice time to leave the party used to be thirty minutes after coffee was served in the living room. Today there may be no such room—nowhere to go. Still, serve coffee to signal the event is almost over.

HOW: When no one wants to get up, but you want to declare the party done, stop serving or pouring. If cutting off the alcohol doesn't work, simply begin talking about the evening in the past tense: "What a great night this was!" Which is to say, "We're done here." Be clear, and they may get the point.

NOTHING WORKS: If everyone is having a good time, the party shouldn't end. Show your guests the drinks supply, put out some snacks, and hop off to bed.

SEVEN

Not your Party

If you're going to play the game properly, you'd
better know every rule.
—Barbara Jordan

Very little is about you at someone else's dinner party
except your table manners.

MANNERS FROM RSVP TO ATTENDING

RSVP

Remember that replying "yes" to an invitation does not
suddenly make it your party. Whatever expectations you
may have, make sure they match what you've heard from
the host. If there's a big difference, find a way to decline
politely. Here's how.

NO, THANKS: Giving a reason for "no" isn't necessary, but may help lessen hurt feelings. Keep the dying grandmothers to a minimum. "Overwhelmed at the moment" is understood by all.

MAYBE: Just say yes or no.

WRITTEN INVITATION: Mail back an RSVP card, but, given the sluggishness of snail mail, follow up with a text, an e-mail, or a call.

Add-Ons

The more may be the merrier, but that's not your call as a guest.

ASSUME: Anyone not invited is not invited. This saves you from being turned down when you ask to bring your kids. If a babysitter cancels, call the host to cancel, leaving it to the host to say, "Don't be silly, bring the kids."

NO, BUT . . . : If going with "I have a houseguest, so I can't come," know the difference between the host's "I will not hear of them not coming as well" and "I think it would be all right for you to bring them." The "think" is a plea for you to opt out.

DON'T SURPRISE: Kids, lovers, mothers, pets (except service dogs), and houseguests are not necessarily invited because you would like them to be. A good host will jump through hoops to make an unannounced guest feel welcome, but do you really want to see the jumping?

Gifts

To avoid last-minute work for the hosts, bring a present that does not have to do with the event, something personal that they love and can enjoy on their own time. You know they love Chinese white tea? Bring a pound of the best one you can afford.

CANDY: Not unless you know they really want it. Fine when Jean Harlow lounged in bed in a white fox fur wrap and caribou stork feathered slippers and ate a box of chocolates without gaining an ounce. That's Hollywood, not us.

FLOWERS: Be sure to send either before or after the occasion, because what's the host going to do with a bunch of flowers at the door when other guests have to be greeted and introduced? If you must, make sure they are already in a vase with water.

WINE: As much of a no-brainer as a bottle of wine might seem, therein lies its downfall: very little thought. What's the host going to do with a bottle, other than wonder whether to serve it, keep it, or give it away? Some etiquette authorities say the host must serve the wine so as not to look like he or she doesn't like it, doesn't care, or is greedy and ungenerous. Why put anyone in that position?

Arriving

EARLY: There is no such thing as being fashionably early. Nothing puts a host off his stride more than an early guest. Walk around the block, go to the mall—anything—or treat this as the perfect time to check your e-mails and make calls, so you don't have to for the next two and a half hours.

ON TIME: One can assume that when a host says the party starts at seven-thirty she doesn't intend to serve the food on the dot. But you still have only ten minutes without ruffling the host's feathers.

LATE: Late is late, but when it's unavoidable, contact the host and give an estimated time for your arrival. If you're likely to be very late, ask something like "Might it be better if I don't come?" If the answer is to get there when you can, leave it at that. The host is too busy for more conversation.

CANCELING: If you are a senior staffer in the White House, canceling at the last minute is a given. For the rest of us, any host needs at least a day's notice of your cancellation. Unless you have something infectious. In that case, never go.

"WHAT'S TO EAT?": This seemingly innocent inquiry undoes all the good you achieved by complimenting the dog. Don't expect the host who is long past the menu stage of the meal to go through that spiel with everyone.

DRINKS: The host is busy. No matter if he or she makes the first drink for you; make sure it's the last he or she has to. Unless there are servers, make the next one yourself.

SOCIALIZE: Even if you're not a good mixer, help get the room going so the host can concentrate on the food and wine and on getting everyone to the table on time.

At the Table

WHEN TO SIT: The time to sit is whenever the host invites everyone to the table, whether the places are already marked, the host tells each guest where to sit, or he or she just says, "Sit wherever you like."

GRACE: Let the host do whatever he or she wants. You don't have to do anything but keep quiet or join in.

WHO STARTS: If the host tells you to start as soon as there's a plate in front of you, then do. If he or she doesn't, wait until he or she starts, or a lot of people at the table do.

ELBOWS ON THE TABLE: The train of the old rule about never putting your elbows on the table left the station a long time ago: as long as you aren't eating while you put them there, and as long as the host is occasionally doing the same thing.

STANDING: It may be unnecessary for men to get up from the table whenever a woman does these days. Follow the host's lead. We wouldn't want him to feel lonely.

NAPKINS: When the host picks up his or her napkin, that's the signal to pick up yours. The eating begins. Picking up yours the moment you sit down is fine, too, unless you are at Buckingham Palace, where you have to wait for the Queen to touch hers. When you leave, gather it together neatly and leave it on whatever side you are handed.

BREAD DUNKING: See chapter 4, "How to Eat" (page 27), for the full Monty. If the sauce on the peppered filet mignon is full of Madeira and butter, grab a small piece of bread and dunk. You are showing your appreciation for good food. Why would any host object to that?

NEED SOMETHING: Want the salt? If you can get it without more than your forearm crossing the edge of the table, reach for it. If you might knock over your neighbor's wine, ask to have it passed. And when you pass it, make sure you include the pepper as well—half the work for twice the effect.

I CAN'T EAT THAT

There is a difference between an ingredient you don't like and one that will kill you. No one is worth dying for, but personal dislikes at someone else's table should be endured with style. When a bowl of garlic mayonnaise is placed on the host's summer lunch table to go with the platter

of vegetables, a loud exclamation, "I LOATHE GAR-LIC," is bratty. It upsets the tone of the event and puts the other guests on edge. No one is forcing it on you, and if they are, a "No, thank you," is all you need to keep the garlic off your plate. If it's already on your plate, just don't eat it.

Allergic or in Danger

Pregnant and can't eat raw fish or meat? Nuts will make you stop breathing? If a food or beverage health threat is real and serious, inform your host very specifically what it is, preferably when you accept the invitation.

Bugs

Some multi-legged creature sharing your salad? No shrieks, just a quiet dispatch into your napkin or onto the side of the plate if it's not crawling. Why embarrass the host or put an overly sensitive guest off his food?

Compliments

Complimenting the food makes the host happy. If you can't eat one thing, praise another.

Raw or Undercooked

Some people cannot eat raw food for health reasons. Others just don't like it. In the latter case, the host's definition of medium rare may be your rare, but it's best to keep quiet.

If undercooked food is dangerous for you and others, it's not enough just to push the food around the plate, as good table manners usually require. Be brave, and quietly but quickly tell your host.

HELPING OUT

Offering to help is exercising your manners. Good manners is actually doing it. Great manners is doing it with minimum harassment to the host. Bottom line is, when you say it, mean it. Better to say, "May I help you with the . . . ?" and say something specific than simply "May I help?"

Alcohol

The consequences of any guest drinking too much may end up being everyone's responsibility, not just the host's. Especially when one of the guests is too drunk to drive or walk home safely. It may take more than the host to cajole the guest and get the keys. If the guest is manageable, offer to take him or her home if it's not impossibly out of your way, or help call a taxi. The host will love you.

Food

Start with the obvious. Is the garlic peeling itself? Are glasses, knives, and forks leaping onto the table and corks flying out of their bottles? If the host is spinning the salad, offer to take over.

Dishes

Don't everyone jump up and race the dishes into the sink, where they don't belong. Leave the dishwasher alone unless you're clearly asked to fill it. No host wants to watch all this chaos.

When

The general rule is that pitching in is admirable as long as you don't make the host wish you weren't. Showing someone how to help is often more work than simply doing it yourself. Look around. Offering to open the wine when you see the bottles on the counter with a corkscrew next to them is perfect.

SMOKING

Ask where to smoke. Don't presume you can and don't just disappear out into the snowbank.

THE END

The end of eating is when the host puts his or her napkin on the table after the last course and coffee. If that hasn't worked, the absence of more wine being poured is another clue.

Eat and Run

What keeps you in good stead and invited back is leaving ten to twenty minutes after you have finished your tea or coffee, whenever or wherever it's served.

Endless Goodbyes

Restrict your goodbyes to how much you enjoyed the party, so you don't keep the host from washing up and falling into bed.

Leaving Before the End

If the party is running late and you have to get up at four in the morning to catch a flight, it's fine to say you just have to go. And relieving babysitters trumps all.

THANK-YOU NOTES

A thank-you is due within twenty-four hours. A written note is a less daunting task if you have the stationery and stamps in advance. All you need then is to use a decent pen, to be able to write legibly, and to know how to mail it the next day.

Pronto, Please

No one objects to a telephone call or an e-mail before receiving the note. Just mention that a proper note will follow.

What to Say

You don't have to be Shakespeare. A simple thanks and adoration are sufficient. Talk about what most impressed you, but always say something nice about the food and company. All the host really wants to know is if you had a good time. No seeking reassurances. If you were caught giving a steak bone to the Great Dane at the table without asking first, then add a brief apology and leave it at that. Don't ask to be forgiven; you are just making more work for your host.

EIGHT

Restaurants

**The world was my oyster, but
I used the wrong fork.
—Oscar Wilde**

Here's how to use the right fork when out and about.

PICKING A PLACE

Host

ACCESS: Are there stairs or raised areas, or is the private dining upstairs with no elevator? Knowing all these in advance saves a lot of last-minute hassle and embarrassment, for both the host and any guests with physical restrictions.

DRESS CODE: Find out in advance if there is one. Pay particular attention to ties, jeans, and jackets. Alert your guests when inviting them.

NOISE: Know the noise level. Find out if anyone is hard of hearing.

RESTAURANT: Your choice is all about the guests' having a good time. The best chance of success is to go to a restaurant you already know and where they know you.

THE BILL: Is it your bill, or is everyone paying his or her own? Will the restaurant split the check? Do everyone a favor and let your guests know when you invite them.

Guest

DRESS CODE: Check online so you aren't embarrassed when you get there to find there's a code you don't fit. That being said, personal style within certain boundaries (no sweatpants or grungy clothing) is fine if you're comfortable in your own style and can carry it off.

EXPENSE: If everyone is paying separately and the venue is too expensive, say so. Everyone knows you might rather put that extra money toward a vacation than spend it on an eighty-dollar steak. No time to be a hero.

MAKING SUGGESTIONS: It's only okay to ask why the host picked the place if you know him or her extremely well. "If you want lobster, I know an even better place; the lobsters arrive every day and are not from a dirty tank" will come off as rude unless a close friendship is already established.

MENU: Look at the menu online, so hemming and hawing at the table is cut to a minimum. There are few things more annoying than a guest who cannot make up his or her mind and keeps all the others waiting.

SO YOU DON'T LIKE IT: Unlike Ann Landers's preventive cure for pregnancy, "An aspirin held firmly between the knees," there's nothing to do if you don't like the choice of restaurant. Simply join the party and tap into your reservoir of manners.

ARRIVING

Host

EARLY: Arrive early, to check in with the dining room or bar manager. Make sure all your arrangements are known and accounted for, and that your server has been alerted to any special needs.

PAYING: Leaving your card with the greeter when you arrive makes for a seamless event. Make sure the staff knows who's paying, especially if you are a woman. Otherwise, the staff may give the check to the seemingly most prosperous or eldest male.

Guest

DON'T BE LATE: It's Friday night and you're taking a cab in the rain? Plan on being fifteen minutes early or you may be that late.

FIRST TO ARRIVE: Tell the name of the host to the person at the reception desk. It may be restaurant policy that you can't go to the table until the party is complete. Better to go to the bar, look at the menu, get an idea of the prices if you are paying your share, and have fun anticipating what you will eat.

THE BAR

Host

CROWDING: Herd any of your guests in the bar away from it to clear access for others. Bar fights ruin the digestion.

THE CHECK: Make clear who is paying before the first round of drinks to avoid a lot of "What just happened back there?" as everyone leaves the bar.

Guest

BE CONSIDERATE: Once you have your drink, step far away from the bar. Others need to get to it, and you don't want to force them to use their elbows to move you and your drink out of the way. Have mercy on the bartender's time by not insisting on a smoke machine for your Manhattan when ten others are waiting for a simple glass of chardonnay. And it's very nice for the host if you pay your bar bill before going to the table, even if the bartender says he or she will transfer it.

THE TABLE

Host

GETTING TO THE TABLE: In a group, you should lead, since you will need to direct the seating. Or be already at the table to greet your guests and direct them.

UNSATISFIED: Don't like the table? Ask if it can be changed. Do this before sitting down. Once you are seated, it's way too late; you don't want to ask everyone to get up again. Unless there are bike messengers whizzing by— then everyone will want to.

Guest

DISPLEASED: Unless you are in physical danger, it's not up to you to ask for a different table. Suffer with a smile, and no one else will have to feel your pain.

PLEASED: If you do like the table, compliment the host, and good feelings will continue. Food always tastes better that way.

THE STAFF

Host

SERVERS: It's the host's job to make sure everything goes smoothly with the servers. Classic ways to make sure it doesn't: snapping your fingers to get the servers' attention will probably make them head away from the

table and stay there; rattling the ice in your "empty" glass will do the same.

Guest

SERVERS: I have read the etiquette rule "Don't talk to the waiter." Nonsense. Why interrupt the host if you need more water or butter, the server is passing by, and you have the chance to ask him or her without disrupting the table? That being said, no matter how slow you think the service is, correcting it or even drawing attention to it is not up to you. That's the host's job.

DRINKS

Please don't bring up the old rag about cocktails destroying one's palate. So does toothpaste, but a Negroni is a lot more fun.

Host

INITIAL OFFER: "Would anyone like a cocktail?" is the important opener to your guests. If everyone has been to the bar already, it's "Another?"

LETTING GUESTS CHOOSE: Offer wines by the glass before you find out what everyone is eating. Then guests can choose the wine that goes with what they are ordering.

Guest

COCKTAILS: If no drinks are offered, you are out of luck. Unless you know the host very well and are sure that he or she has forgotten to ask. Then ask.

ORDERING

Host

COURSES: The seamless way to start the ordering is for the host to say how many courses he or she is having. This saves a lot of time and tedious group discussion. The group should be in accord about how many courses everyone will have, so some are not going to be left with empty forks.

PRICE: Want everyone to have that three-pound lobster? Simply say, "Look at that lobster. Anyone who wants it, please have it."

SPECIAL REQUESTS: Don't ask for a birthday cake at the last minute, though the kitchen can often do something festive, and some restaurants like to make a show of it. If you have some other request for food not on the menu, keep it reasonable and without fuss. Power ordering is not actual power, it's just showing off, and these days annoyingly obsessive.

TASTING MENU: Same as for the number of courses. "Shall we have the tasting menu?" or "The main courses look so good, why don't we all order what we want?" settles that.

Guest

INTERRUPTING THE SERVER: Talking while the server is taking orders means he or she might have to repeat the list of specials. Again. When the same questions have to be answered endlessly, everyone will wish they had stayed home. Nothing you have to say is more important than the other guests' getting their orders in so the table can then relax and continue their conversations.

PRICE: Eyeing that three-pound lobster? Don't order it unless it's in the price range of courses the host has suggested, or unless he or she has encouraged all to order it.

SPECIAL REQUESTS: For the server alone to hear. Don't interrupt the others while deciding things like whether to hold the sauce or add a side of asparagus.

WINE

Wine selection falls to the host. A polite guest enjoys whatever's provided.

Host

ORDERING: Take control of choosing the wines, but keep your ears open for someone at the table whose advice can be helpful.

PRICE: Price is no guaranteed guide to drinking satisfaction. If the thirty-dollar-per-bottle range is your desired price range and you don't want to broadcast that to the table, open the wine list and point to others in the same price range. The waiter or sommelier will understand. If you want to splurge and don't want to pick an expensive dud, point to a higher price on the list and say, "I would like your best chardonnay in that range."

TASTING: For some, all that noisy sucking and slurping through the teeth means they think they look like they know what they are doing and are real pros. It doesn't. It's just noisy. If this is your first time tasting wine at a restaurant, simply take a sip and, unless it's vinegar, say "That's fine, thank you."

WHEN THE HOST DOESN'T LIKE: Tasting the wine is to see if it has any problems, not whether you like it. If in doubt, ask the server or sommelier to taste it, too.

Guest

WHEN THE GUEST DOESN'T LIKE: Only the host can decide if the wine is crap. Whether you love red and the host orders white or vice versa, the host's selection is final. Massive cabernets give you a headache? If that's the case, explain it quietly and tell your host that you would prefer to order something by the glass.

TABLE ISSUES

Anything that interrupts the social and gastronomic flow of the meal is unwelcome. Keeping disturbances to a minimum makes for a party everyone will want to repeat.

Doggie Bags

That Porterhouse steak bone is very hard to leave behind. Unless a formal or business occasion, ask for the bag. It can be a late-night snack for you or the dog. If you find yourself suddenly ill and needing to leave, take the whole course if you can face the smell of it in the taxi.

Don't Like the Food

If everyone agrees, and you are the host, send it back and replace it. If a guest, and alone in your problem, best not to make a fuss that would put the others off their food. Push it around until the next course.

Diets

Whatever diet you are on, it's much nicer to others to keep it to yourself. If you don't want to finish the food, just leave it. Don't set up a cross of weight loss and nail yourself to it in public. Frightens the onlookers.

Finished or Not

The progression of the meal will be smooth if everyone finishes each course more or less at the same time. If you find yourself finishing early, leave that last morsel and then scoop it up as everyone else is finishing. Placing the utensils vertically in the center of the plate used to be the final signal you had finished, and many servers still recognize it.

Medicine

This should not come up at the table unless you want to ruin the moment. Take your pills before or after the meal. If you must take them with food, do it when water is poured, and then with a sleight of hand. Almost everyone takes pills, but there's no need to do so ostentatiously.

Panic

You can't read the menu in French; you are asked to choose the wine; the food is weird to you; the chopsticks are plastic and slippery and you can't get a grip on the shrimp. Fess up. Be comfortable telling it like it is and asking for advice. That way you get to eat.

Salt and Pepper

Some food just tastes better if black pepper or salt is ground over it, no matter how good the chef. If brilliant, the chef will do it the second before the food leaves the kitchen. If not, it's up to you to get over any issues about insulting the chef. You are the one paying. Ask for salt and pepper mills.

Sharing

The kitchen sometimes can split an order and sometimes cannot. Splitting a single poached egg is silly and cheap. Splitting a Caesar salad is easily done, and a fine way to start a lunch.

Stomach Rebellion

If it's a burp coming on, a napkin or a handkerchief over the mouth covers it. Literally. If gas, head for the balcony. If nerves make your stomach gurgle and growl, say, "Please excuse my stomach," and then ignore it; that's all you can do. If the whole meal threatens to return, for everyone's sake don't hesitate to head for the bathroom. Say, "Excuse me a moment," and run.

THE CHECK

A friend invited a billionaire to his favorite local café, chosen as much for the owner giving him a price break as for the food. When the check arrived, the host saw that the prices had been adjusted to a Rockefeller level, assuming the billionaire was going to pay. The Rockefeller was probably used to this; after glancing at the bill, he slipped the host some cash under the table without comment, and without anyone else's noticing. Manners at their best.

Dating

In the past, it was always the man who paid, but now he might not be the one carrying the flushest credit card, or maybe there are two men, or none. You invite, you pay. Unless other arrangements have been made in advance, and that should be very clear. If it's clear who is picking up the check, the other can offer to buy drinks at the bar before going to the table. A small gesture like this goes a long way.

Pretending

Don't fake wanting to pay with "Is it my turn?," because whose turn it is should be clear when you accept the invitation. That clumsy reach for the check, making motions of getting out your credit card, can taint what has otherwise been a fine time. Enjoy the benefits of contemporary manners. Feel at ease to say, "Shall we both pay, or will you?" if the person who invited you is slow on the draw.

Splitting Checks in Large Groups

To save time, tell the server up front. Cash is fastest; ten credit cards could take a while and might be unwelcome.

TIPPING

Remember that the take-home money earned by the service staff, except for minimum wage, is not paid out of the cost of the meal. The servers and others count on your tip to live. But you do have options.

How Much

If you are really happy with the service, leave a tip of 20 percent. Ecstatic because the server performed brilliantly and made the evening? Then 25 percent or more.

Included

Look to see if the service tip is included, unless you want to fork out 35 percent or more. If the tip is included, it's considerate to leave anything that picks up the slack from the 15-percent rate added to your bill. Even if 20 percent was added, if you're really happy with the service, leave an additional 2 to 5 percent. As far as the server is concerned, cash is king.

No Tipping

This is a new policy in some restaurants. Easier on the customer, once everyone is used to it and knows how it works.

Withholding

Remember that if the food isn't good it's not the server's fault. Unless he or she screwed up the ordering and timing and ruined the kitchen's best efforts.

Host Under-Tips

No party can be a success with the guests embarrassed because a host has under-tipped. If he or she under-tips, and if you're at one of your favorite restaurants and you can afford to, you might want to rectify that—the next day.

FOR THE SERVER

These are some guidelines for being the best server you can be and for making the most money, but they may run counter to your training in any given restaurant. Management may want you to give your name, may want you to clear each plate as it is emptied, etc. If you can read the table accurately, and you sense clearly what kind of service those customers want, then put a toe in the water with restraint; if they smile, then continue—of course, out of hearing or sight of the management. After all, the customer is paying, not your boss. But remember, just because one table loves one type of service does not mean the next one will. Try to read each table, if you can.

The Table

This is your domain. Pay attention before the customers arrive that all is clean, in order, all there, and ready to impress. Are all the glasses sparkling? The utensils spotless? And nothing brings a just-seated party down faster than a table that wobbles and spills the host's or anyone's favorite cocktail.

Introductions

Not necessary. The guests are the host's priority when they sit down, not the server's name. So don't announce it. If the host cares what it is, he or she will ask. If the guests do, they will.

What's Available

Know what foods on the menu and what wines on the list are not available. Inform everyone up front. The customer's excitement and anticipation at seeing one of his or her favorite dishes can turn into real anger when the server comes back to the table after all the orders are in to announce it doesn't exist. Inexcusable.

Specials

Keep the speech about specials to a lean minimum. The customer wants the server to get to the point, not a recipe. If the customers care what farm the lamb comes from, they will ask. They certainly don't want to hear endless descriptions again as the server recites the same evening's specials bible to the surrounding tables. Hearing that the recommended wine smells to you like fallen leaves will raise the customer's blood pressure, and the point of being at a restaurant is to lower it.

Know the Food and Wine

The customers don't want long speeches about the cocktails, food, and wine, whereas they do want the server to know how to answer questions about ingredients. Either know definitely or find out. Never guess.

Don't Abandon the Table

Give the customers a cocktail, some wine, water, bread, anything, in the first five to ten minutes of their sitting down. Ten minutes is stretching it, so if it's taken that long you will have to work harder after that. If the host ordered a white wine and there is no cold bottle of that one available, *tell him or her*, then bring an ice bucket with the bottle in it immediately. Ask if the customer would like a glass of a similar wine in the meantime. If you as the server can't get to it fast, get a busser or another server to do it. Use your team. Keep the customer informed.

Wine Service

Fast and easy, please. Show the customer the bottle, and know if the vintage is the same as he or she ordered. The host may be in conversation and forget to notice. Show the label. To taste the wine properly, whoever ordered the wine will need at least an ounce or two in the glass. When the wine is approved, fill glasses only to the level of where the angle of the glass turns inward. No more, no less. Only then can the customers swirl the wine if they want to appreciate it fully. Don't touch the glass with your hands except by the stem. Warm hands on my cold wine are not welcome.

Who Ordered What

Know before approaching a table with the plates of food who has ordered what. Don't ask, "Who's having the ravioli?"— you should know. The question catches the guests off guard and interrupts the feeling and tone at the table.

"Enjoying the Food?"

Aren't you and the chef supposed to know better than the customers when the food is perfect and when it isn't?

When the first forkful is poised to enter their mouths, what do you expect them to say? Once they've tasted the food, if it's awful, they will get your attention. Try to look at each table as often as you can, so you notice when they are trying to catch your eye. But it's also up to you to figure out if the customers want to chat with you. If so, chat away.

Clearing Plates

A very tricky question is when to clear the plates. The world seems divided on this. I'm in the camp that says never clear the plates until everyone has finished. But trust the customer on this. If the host wants a plate cleared when it's empty, regardless of the others, he or she will let you know. Then it's better to do it.

The Check

Asking for the check means the customer wants to pay and leave. The host gets to judge this, and once he or she has asked for it, the group is ready to go. Don't make them wait to see you again for fifteen minutes after the check has been dropped.

Tipping

If service is included, say so. If it isn't and the customer has had too much wine and either forgets or miscalculates the tip, you or a manager can point that out, if you're able to find a safe and polite way to do so.

FOR EVERYONE

Below is advice for host *and* guests at a restaurant. Going out with friends spontaneously? Then you are host and guest. Here are three good rules regardless of whether you are host, guest, or both.

Volume

Unless you are in a noisy bar, use your indoor voice. Spare other tables any overbearing volume.

Be Kind to the Staff

They are serving you. They are not your servants. Treat them as you like to be treated in your professional life.

Mistakes

Finally, everyone makes mistakes. If your server forgets something or spills something, be gracious and understanding. And if you don't like your food, no need to behave like the judge on a reality cooking show and insult the chef. Just explain that it's not to your taste, and ask to order something else.

NINE

Eating ON THE GO

> Has food on the American planes . . . improved?
> It has not in Europe, it is incredibly bad, even
> worse than on trains. Do they cook these meals
> in the locomotive and in the fuselage?
> —*The Alice B. Toklas Cook Book*

As rampant as eating on the go is in America, you don't want to be caught mid-step, mid-bite, and also mid-embarrassment. Table manners don't apply only when a table is present.

BEACHES AND PARKS

Leave scenic areas as you found them, or better. Good for health, the environment, and your karma. The seagulls will clean up any crumbs you left, but not the wrappers.

BED-AND-BREAKFASTS

You may be required to talk to strangers at a communal table for breakfast. If that's a shock beyond your comprehension, take a tray to your room. Explain that you can't talk before ten, or before you've had your coffee.

BOATS

Be sure to drink less alcohol than on land, unless you don't mind falling overboard.

ELEVATORS

Who wants his nose and clothes assaulted by someone's industrial-food-complex pepperoni? Or wants to have it all over the back of his coat when the elevator comes to a rushing stop at the hundredth floor? Nobody. Wait to eat until you've arrived at your destination.

PLANES

Just because U.S. airlines have turned to barbarism doesn't mean you have to. Once you're in your seat, it's too late to wonder why you brought smelly, messy, spillable food with you. Raw garlic may be ambrosia to you, but smelly clouds of it spreading over the rows around you may not be to anyone else.

As for drinks, at even a hint of turbulence, pick up your cup from the ice-slick fold-down tray in front of you. That little indentation to hold it in place is a mirage. Keeping your Bloody Mary and sweet, creamy coffee off your neighbor at the beginning of a ten-hour flight is a nice thing.

SHIPS

Manners on ships are all about how you behave to the staff. Treat them right and you will get manners back and the vacation you've dreamed of. If you want service in your stateroom, in the dining room, or at the bar to be beyond your expectations, be sure to seek out whoever is in charge of that area and tip largely. Ordering champagne or canapés for your arrival alerts the staff that you know what you're doing. Nothing gets around a ship faster.

TAXIS

Eating in a taxi is understandable only if you are taking one from Jersey to San Francisco. But if you are on a short ride and absolutely must, keep your breakfast in the bag and eat carefully over the opening of the bag, so the next passenger doesn't slide in over a seat drenched in coffee, milk, sugar, and doughnut debris. Taking your trash with you is essential.

THEATERS AND MOVIES

Opening a giant bag of potato chips and spending the next thirty minutes crunching or sucking down a two-quart Diet Coke is a sure way to ruin the movie for those around you. Open snacks before entering the theater or during the previews, and be conscious of slurping when you hit the dregs of your beverage.

TEN

Techiquette

> For a list of all the ways technology has failed to
> improve the quality of life, please press 3.
> —Alice Kahn, *Multiple Sarcasm*

It would seem that technology has completely defaced the world of table manners, but in actuality little has changed. When bringing technology to the table, just remember that what's important, and always has been, is to make those around you feel that you are engaged and want to be there. Keep in mind that staring at your phone doesn't make you look less awkward and more popular, it makes you unapproachable.

It is increasingly fashionable to say that technology and social media have disconnected everyone and manners no longer matter, that no one really cares much beyond him- or herself. But sometimes these things remind us that manners work to bring people together. An awkward cocktail hour without your smartphone is simply that, just one hour.

TAKING AND MAKING CALLS DURING A MEAL

Business Calls

There isn't a host or plus-one out there who enjoys hearing, "I need to take this," every two seconds. If there's an emergency in the office, absolutely step out. If you know things are going awry prior to the event, it may be best to cancel and head to the office to put out fires, rather than disrupting the other guests, who aren't getting paid to solve or endure this week's work fiasco.

Emergency

The test of a true personal emergency is when everyone would agree it is. If you know in advance that something might happen, tell the host or your guests that you might be checking your phone or ducking out.

Headphones

A fine way to escape, but not at the dinner table, cocktails, or a party.

Keep It Down or Leave the Room

Others around the table or at a cocktail party probably already know about the latest news headline and certainly don't want to get a debriefing on the doctor's appointment you just left. They don't want to hear about your tragic breakup, either. If you must talk on the phone, leave the room, or at least find a quiet corner and cup your other hand over your mouth when you talk. Better yet, what's so important that it can't wait?

Speakerphone

There really is no need unless Grandma Joan, who just had a hip replacement and wasn't able to attend, calls to say hello to the whole family. Otherwise, follow the guidelines above for "Keep It Down or Leave the Room." In other words: keep it down or leave the room.

Vigilante Action

Whether it's a host or a guest, if someone's cell-phone barbarism is disrupting the whole event, any of your politer versions of "Would you please shut up?" work well.

TEXTING

Go ahead and text, but keep in mind that texting can exclude you from those around you, and them from you. Not always the interesting and successful choice. If you find yourself unable to put your phone down, it may be a sign that you aren't having fun or would rather be hanging out with others, in which case it will be politer to excuse yourself than to kill the atmosphere by acting bored and uninterested.

There are a few exceptions. You want to text Dave because everyone is sad he had to miss the event for a family function? Fine. You and your partner want to check in quickly with the kids? Also fine. If you're hanging out with a close friend for the fourth time that week, maybe it's understood that within a few minutes you'll both be on your phones, still enjoying each other's silent company. Use your judgment, keeping in mind what situations are isolating versus inclusive or essential.

SOCIAL MEDIA

Being plugged in but checked out doesn't contribute to any kind of party or social gathering. Here is when it does—and does not.

Facebook

If it feels irresistible to put event photos on Facebook, keep in mind that what's amusing and of interest to you may not be to the host (if he wanted everyone in on the details of the event, he would have invited them), or to those who were left out of the party. If you care that an uninvited friend may be hit with a serious case of FOMO (Fear of Missing Out), then don't put them up. If any photos involve obviously compromising situations, ask permission

first. People might love you for it, but going viral for some may be as much fun as a dose of Ebola.

Instagram

Feeling the need to 'gram a selfie of you and an old friend you ran into at the gala, or a mouthwatering shot of your plated main course, to share with friends and followers? Before you Instagram with abandon, ask yourself two things: Am I inconveniencing anyone by holding my phone at arm's length to take a selfie? Best not to knock the hundred-dollar lobster out of the server's hands as he goes to serve it. And am I just doing this to make others jealous? If the answer is yes to either of these questions, best to keep your photos to yourself. As for taking pictures of every dish, if they can be done quickly, without disrupting the service and without annoying the other guests, then go for it.

Live Tweeting

Live tweeting may be exactly what a host wants, or his or her worst nightmare. If you are at a charity cocktail party, a restaurant opening, or any other event where publicity and attention are essential for success, and you have the host's active permission, then go crazy. If not, it's an unforgivable invasion of privacy, especially at an intimate dinner party.

INTERRUPTIONS

Google It

It's tempting to look up the "right" answer to your table's debate on who was thought most likely to win the 1948 presidency, but keep in mind that this will conclude the conversation. And once you pull out your phone, others will, too, dissolving what may have been a lovely conversation into a frenzy of checking texts, e-mails, and other notifications.

Phones on the Table

If you need to have your cell phone on the table, make sure the screen is facing downward, so that as it lights up with notifications the guests around you aren't distracted. And silencing your cell phone is not reserved for movie theaters. No one wants to hear your bells and whistles.

Pictures and Videos

If you wouldn't bring a photo album of your nephew to the table, then maybe it's not the time to scroll through twenty photos of him on your phone for the other guests. Same with video clips. If another guest hands you his or her phone to look at a series of pictures, scroll only forward and never backward, to avoid invading his or her privacy.

HOUSE RULES

What the host says goes. So, if cell phones are collected at the door, or you are politely requested not to post event photos to social media, then go along with it. After all, it's not your party.

Cell Phones

It is increasingly accepted for the host to restrict the use of cell phones at an event. If you are the host, you might ask your guests as they enter. Or have a sign asking them please to turn off their phones until they leave. Or seat a guest near an exit if he or she knows a long call will be coming through.

Social Media

If you want your event all over Instagram's Explore or everyone's Facebook newsfeed, say nothing to your guests. If you don't, say so. Announce to them when they are invited that, for reasons of national security, you don't want any social media photos to appear. Everyone will laugh, and some might even go along with it.

ELEVEN

Pretentious or Not?

A nose too far in the air misses the aroma of the truffles in the hamburger.

In defining what is pretentious and what isn't, context and intention are everything. Was the Pump Room in Chicago pretentious for parading flaming swords of shish kebab through the dining room all night to its enraptured guests? No. That was what they did best, what their guests wanted, and it defined the restaurant. When I put out my grandmother's old American silver, I am having fun and paying homage. It's pretentious only if I am trying to show off or establish social or financial hierarchy. So here's how to deal with some party rituals that may be uncomfortably unfamiliar.

BUTLERS

Butlers are very pretentious and affected if the host doesn't have them around all the time. Caterers and their servers will do.

CANDLES

Votive

Candles can make the mood of a room, partnering with flowers and lighting. The three together are a quick way to dress up a room easily and often inexpensively. Moderation is not the rule here, since quantity works when using the votive size—but not when candelabra are dominating the table so densely you can't see the guests across the table.

Scented

An affectation if scented with anything other than beeswax. Why stink up the room with cheap industrial vanilla smoke when it should be perfumed with the aromas of good food? That's why you are there.

CENTERPIECES

The guide here is whether the centerpiece fits the occasion and whether anyone at the table will appreciate it. If the centerpiece is a huge, expensive Meissen soup tureen

and everyone has ham sandwiches instead of soup, the host has gone over the top.

FINGER BOWLS

These are sometimes considered old-fashioned and pretentious, but are actually very useful and practical, and only pretentious when presented with food that does not require them.

What They Are

Small, usually glass or silver bowls almost filled with lukewarm water scented with lemon slices or flower petals. A practical necessity when the food served is to be eaten with one's fingers. A way to make everyone comfortable. Saves napkins, too.

When to Serve

Traditionally, just before dessert, in case your fingers have some of the previous course on them. Logically, these bowls should be presented anytime guests have just eaten with their fingers. Why suffer through a course with sticky fingers just because the etiquette-dictated time for finger bowls has not arrived? That is etiquette at its silliest.

How to Deal with Them

Watch the host or hostess. Do what he or she does. Don't drink from the bowl even if your water glass is empty, or unless you want someone to tell that hackneyed and apocryphal Queen Victoria story. (Okay, okay: she drank from hers to make a guest comfortable who had already done that.)

The bowl will arrive on a plate with or without a doily or small napkin under it. If it's before dessert, the plate will later receive the dessert dish. Lift up the bowl and the doily/napkin and put it where your bread plate was, at the top left of your table setting. The old rule is to use the finger bowl once, but ignore that. Wash as stickiness demands. And just before leaving the table, because it feels good. Leave the bowl where it is.

FLOWERS

There are too many flowers when the guests can't see one another. Keep the flowers low or high enough so that the guests aren't leaning over sideways to talk to the people across from them. Keep the cut orchids under a few dozen unless you are in California or Hawaii. Otherwise, it's the same as parking a Ferrari in the room.

LARGE NAPKINS

Many consider large napkins an affectation, but they can be very useful. A whole lobster can send juices flying, most of them on you. Show you are confident with your table manners and tuck the napkin in at the top of your shirt whenever you want. This keeps dry-cleaning expenses under control, and the rarely used black or white tie will be ready for action once more. Hiding the pearls is a bit extreme, so tuck the napkin into the top of your dress.

MENU TERMS

The same dish can be down-home or pretentious, depending on what you call it and in what language. The time for French terms in American-cuisine restaurants has gone the way of required ties for men and hats for women.

Appetizer or Hors d'Oeuvre
In French, "hors d'oeuvre," but not when you mean a first course; the term means "outside the list of dishes on the menu." Since there is only one menu, there is never an "s" on "oeuvre" even if there are lots of them. But back to the "appetizer," which in England is a "starter." Why not just stick to "first course"? Whatever it's called, it is supposed to wake up the appetite and get it going before the full menu begins.

Amuse-Bouche
Usually a bite-sized bit of something that is offered before the first course arrives, an "appetizer" that stimulates a desire for and anticipation of the food to follow. Avoid all

affectation and mispronunciations and just call it that: an appetizer.

Entrée

Traveling abroad, you will find this term means a small course served before the larger one. In a French restaurant, painful confusion can take hold. Hard to pin down pretension in all this confusion, but "entrée" in America is an affectation. Just say "main course" and leave it at that.

PALATE CLEANSER

A palate cleanser is a break over the course of the meal to give one's palate a rest, sometimes a sorbet or sherbet, often called an "intermezzo." Whatever it's called, all that untimely ice is a vicious attack on one's palate and a fraudulent attempt to put class into a meal. Just serving it shows that you don't know what you are doing.

If you insist on an intermezzo in your menu, the only nonaggressive restorative is consommé. Nothing works like a little cup of chicken soup.

PEPPERMILLS

The only point of huge peppermills in a restaurant is so that no one can easily steal them. When they are used to announce fine dining, they are not only pretentious, but ridiculous as they are flourished around the room.

SPECIAL IMPLEMENTS

Fish Knives and Forks

Presenting fish knives and forks with boneless fish is ludicrously affected and pretentious. But when a whole fish with bones shows up, it's necessary and therefore not pretentious at all.

HOW: First cut down along the center from the head to the tail. Using the flat surface of the knife, slide it between the bone and the top fillet to free this from the backbone. Now the top fillet can be easily eaten. When you're finished with it, push the side fin bones off to the edge of the plate. Slide the knife under the backbone from head to tail to loosen it from the bottom fillet. Lift the backbone up and shove it to the side of the plate, or to a plate that has been provided for discards. Then you have the bottom fillet ready for eating.

Marrow Spoon

It's pretentious to serve a marrow spoon when the marrow is on toast. When it's still in the bone, not using that little scoop of a marrow spoon means you don't get to eat the marrow.

SERVICE PLATES

A fine way to dress a table, but don't flub it by leaving them there past the first course unless there's a good reason, such as serving a soup: everyone needs a place to put the empty spoon. After that, the service plates should be removed, unless they are solid gold and you want to continue to show them off. Then you are showing off.

WRAPPED LEMONS

Putting cheesecloth or cotton clothes on a lemon is not an affectation but, rather, a highly practical courtesy, one that prevents digging for seeds in iced tea, or prevents squirting someone in the eye with lemon juice when all you are trying to do is flavor the fish. It also saves having to remember at formal occasions how to squeeze the half-lemon gracefully against the prongs of a fork.

WINEGLASSES

Large

Large wineglasses are for rich white and big red wines that need the volume to develop their aroma and appearance. What they aren't for is to dress a table simply to show you have them. Pouring your inexpensive but delicious aperitif wine into a large Baccarat glass shows the wine to be just a fling, the glass useless, and you as someone who doesn't understand the nature and purpose of either.

Small
Pouring a fifteen-year-old fine Burgundy into a small glass because you think big glasses are an affectation is 360 degrees of pretension.

TWELVE

Eating AROUND THE World

Karma is a bitch only if you are.

Politeness, when genuinely felt and communicated, has no cultural or geographic boundaries. Traveling in an unfamiliar land is difficult enough without running headfirst into a taboo you had no idea existed. Learn what not to do when eating and avoid the worst of possible faux pas.

COMMON SENSE

As a child traveling in Ceylon, Bombay, and Rome, I nearly died three times from not noticing that no one around me was drinking fresh milk. Not knowing other buyers at street vendor stalls were taking it home to boil, I drank it on the spot. After the third event, my blasé mother told the doctors, "Why not just let the little bugger die?" Good point. Self-absorption can kill you.

CONVERSATION

The United States doesn't necessarily have all the answers, so listening more than talking gets you further than not paying attention. Carry a pocket-sized phrase book with phonetic spellings. The rules in chapter 5, "Conversation," apply everywhere, but the more effort you make to learn the local language, the better you'll do.

Slang

The slipperiest slope is trying the local slang. Forget it. You will never get the context right. In Cuba, the Spanish slang equivalent of "Oh, c'mon, you're kidding me," refers in Mexico to a particular version of oral sex. Conservative eighty-year-old grandmothers won't understand why you're asking. And if you use slang ordering your food or drinks, don't be surprised at what turns up. Or when whatever does ends up in your face.

DRINKING

Alcohol

No alcohol drinking in that country? Accept it without any comment. Your hotel will serve you. If not in the lobby, there's always room service.

Coffee and Tea

If everyone around you is drinking these all day and night long, they are probably safe for you as well. Take a moment to find out which of the eight versions of coffee with milk you want, instead of acting as if the barista got your order wrong.

Ice and Water

Not nearly the infectious problem as it used to be. In many countries where no one drinks water from the tap, the ice might be fine, made from the same purified water as bottled. But I would recommend asking where the water came from to make the ice. Is there a sign in your hotel bathroom that says the water isn't safely drinkable? If so, use the bottled. Is bottled water always safe? When the top is sealed, usually. Again, it's not rude to ask, but do so without condescension.

Juices

Freshly squeezed juices are safe, and possibly the best drinks you will ever have—until water or ice is added. If both are safe, then these drinks get even better.

Soft Drinks and Beer

When you see the server opening the can or bottle at the table, appreciate his professionalism. A previously opened bottle may have been filled with something else. If the can of Coke you ordered is not opened in front of you, what's in your glass could be anything brown and fizzy. Stick with beverages you've just seen opened.

EAT IT ALL?

Now that no one knows whether the table is to be cleared all at once or person by person, the signal that you've finished is very important if you want your plate cleared when you have finished eating. But in some places it may not be.

The Food

Some cultures consider it important to finish all the food on your plate; food is not always plentiful or around the next corner. In some cultures it doesn't matter. Look around at other diners.

Unwanted

Pushing the food around as if you are interested can go on only so long before you are found out. Just put your knife and fork together vertically on your plate, or chopsticks on their stand, as if you have finished that course, but not too long before your host does the same thing.

GREETINGS

Effort and a few keys phrases go a long way and make the trip go smoothly.

Hello

Do what you do best. Say "hello" in English if you can't manage the local language without embarrassing yourself. Learn whatever you hear in reply.

Shaking Hands

Shake any hand that's offered first.

Thank You

If there's one phrase to learn in the local language, this is it.

HANDS

Toilet paper has freed up one's left hand for eating in many cultures, though not all. When the custom is to eat from a communal platter with your hands, you can see the point of keeping the left, "toilet" hand away from the food. That way, all can relax and have a fraught-free meal.

Gesturing

Keep your hands out of the air, especially when they're full of knives and forks or chopsticks. Your U.S.A.-innocent gesturing may be misread as panic or aggression.

LEFT

*toilet
hand*

RIGHT

*dining
hand*

HOW TO EAT

Communal

Problems may arise with communal dishes shared with locals. If you're eating from a heaped platter of couscous, it's generally appreciated if you take only what's yours. Wondering which part of the food belongs to each person? It's the "cut-of-the-pie" portion facing you. If there are five pieces of lamb on your cut, it's what you get. No more, unless offered. If in doubt, take time to watch what the locals do, and don't be afraid to ask. Usually, people are happy to show, advise, and help you if you are genuinely interested in doing things their way at the table.

SMOKING

If locals are smoking at the table and you hate it, grin and bear it. But it's okay to move away to the side, or nonaggressively ask the smoker to. However, this problem is unlikely to occur, since these days nonsmoking rules are increasingly common.

SOUNDS

Belching

Whatever guidebooks may tell you about people of certain cultures wanting you to extend thanks in the form of a loud belch after a meal, best forget it, in case you're wrong.

"I'm Stuffed"

Is a gruesome expression in any culture.

Slurping

Slurping noodles in China comes naturally when you have chopsticks, a small bowl, and slippery noodles. The correct way is what you see: bowl held up to the mouth, body bent over the table, and noodles pushed into your mouth with the chopsticks. Sucking in the soup is authentic, but dangerous for beginners. Careful it doesn't go down the wrong way.

Volume

If you want the best service and want to behave well, keep your voice down to the level of the best-behaved local people in the restaurant.

TABOOS

Worldwide tourism has removed most taboos, but it is still best to read a guidebook before your trip. If you can remember all the things not to do when seated in a restaurant, fine. Otherwise, just look around and see what everyone else in the room is doing, as much as you can without staring.

UTENSILS

Chopsticks

Pray for cheap wooden chopsticks that won't slip from your fingers, and a proper chopstick stand so you know where to rest them. If the nearest locals put them down on the place mat still covered in sauce, you are off the hook. Everyone can eat healthfully by ensuring that the mouth end of the chopsticks doesn't go into a communal platter or bowl.

Knives

Old European rules have a knife's cutting edge facing the plate. These days, such subtle signs that you intend no hostility will go unnoticed. It's a nicety you can forget.

Forks

There are endless rules on how to hold them and where to put them before, during, and after eating. Use your good table manners from home, and adjust them to whatever the local person you most admire in the room is doing.

Spoons

Wondering if it's okay to use a spoon wherever you are seems silly once you've eaten Thai food in Thailand without one, picking up slippery sauced cashews with a fork.

Feel comfortable using a spoon, no matter what the stares.

WHEN TO EAT

With jet lag and your internal clock whizzing around at a new and unfamiliar rate, hunger may hit at a time when you can't eat, depending on local customs. It won't do any good to bang on a restaurant door at 6:00 p.m. in Europe. Find a twenty-four-hour café or brasserie for that.

Breakfast

If you are expecting the full show, you had better stay in your hotel. In Europe, don't expect much more than the "Continental" breakfast of orange juice, breads, and tea or coffee.

Lunch

Don't be startled to find restaurants not opening until 1:00 p.m. and the waiters not awake until 2:00 p.m., when they expect the crowd. In many cultures this is the big meal of the day.

Afternoon

In many countries, all the shops are closed from 2:00 to 5:00 or 7:00 p.m. Buy your afternoon snacks, wine, and water before lunch.

Dinner

In Spain, dinner may not get under way until 9:00 p.m., so adjust your eating times to the local clock. In France and Italy, you may not see any locals before 9:00 p.m., but you may get a table.

Conclusion

The most important thing to know about manners is that they're not about you. The more you think about those around you and the less you think about yourself, the more likely you are to behave well. And the better you behave, the more likely you are to be invited back.

SOURCES

Allende, Isabel. *Aphrodite: A Memoir of the Senses*. New York: Harper Perennial, 1999.

The Art of Manliness (blog); www.artofmanliness.com.

Baker, Charles H., Jr. *The Gentleman's Companion*. New York: Crown Publishers, 1946. ("If you ever wondered whose oyster the world is," *Esquire* wrote in 1954, "meet Charles H. Baker, Jr.")

Baldrige, Letitia. *Letitia Baldrige's Complete Guide to the New Manners for the '90s*. New York: Rawson Associates, 1990.

Fenwick, Millicent. *Vogue's Book of Etiquette*. New York: Simon and Schuster, 1948.

Fox, Sue. *Etiquette for Dummies*. Indianapolis: IDG Books, 1999.

Gross-Loh, Christine. "Why Are Hundreds of Harvard Students Studying Ancient Chinese Philosophy?" *Atlantic*, October 8, 2013.

Hoving, Walter. *Tiffany's Table Manners for Teenagers*. New York: Washburn, 1961.

Johnson, Dorothea, and Liv Tyler. *Modern Manners*. New York: Potter Style, 2013.

Junger, Sebastian. "The Bonds of Battle." *Vanity Fair*, June 2015.

Kahn, Alice. *Multiple Sarcasm*. New York: Ten Speed Press, 1985.

Martin, Judith. *Miss Manners' Guide to Excruciatingly Correct Behavior*. New York: W. W. Norton, 2011.

Odessa, Nelly. *99 Rules of Unspoken Social Etiquette: Are You Rude and Don't Even Know It?* New York: Amazon Digital Services, 2012.

SOURCES

Palmer, Diane. "Manners and Etiquette," in *The Dictionary of American History*, 3rd ed. New York: Charles Scribner's Sons, 2002.

Post, Emily. *Etiquette in Society, in Business, in Politics, and at Home.* New York: Funk & Wagnalls, 1922.

Puett, Michael, with Robert Weller, Adam Seligman, and Bennett Simon. *Ritual and Its Consequences: An Essay on the Limits of Sincerity.* Oxford: Oxford University Press, 2008.

Sieberg, Daniel. *The Digital Diet.* New York: Three Rivers, 2011.

Sitwell, Edith. *English Eccentrics.* New York: Penguin Putnam, 1971.

Toklas, Alice B. *The Alice B. Toklas Cook Book.* New York: Harper Perennial, 2010. Originally published 1954.

Vallely, Paul. "Manners makyth man. Etiquette's just nonsense." *Independent,* November 12, 2012; www.independent.co.uk/voices/comment/manners-makyth-man-etiquettes-just-nonsense-8348303.html.

Zinovieff, Sofka. *The Mad Boy, Lord Berners, My Grandmother and Me.* New York: HarperCollins, 2015.

ACKNOWLEDGMENTS

Thanks to: Will Schwalbe of Macmillan, whose idea this book is. Lisa Queen of Queen Literacy Agency, who brought me Will's request to write it. Farrar, Straus and Giroux for publishing it. Bryn Clark for all her invaluable assistance. And to Libby VanderPloeg for making it look so good.

ACKNOWLEDGMENTS

INDEX